Scary Snakes

Vipers

Julie Fiedler

PowerKiDS
press.

New York

Published in 2008 by The Rosen Publishing Group, Inc.
29 East 21st Street, New York, NY 10010

First Edition

Editor: Jennifer Way
Book Design: Julio Gil
Layout Design: Kate Laczynski
Photo Researcher: Nicole Pristash

Photo Credits: Cover, p.1 © www.istockphoto.com/Jim Jurica; pp. 5, 7, 11, 13, 15, 17 © Shutterstock.com; p. 9, 21 © SuperStock, Inc.; p. 19 © Wolfgang Wuster.

Library of Congress Cataloging-in-Publication Data

Fiedler, Julie.
   Vipers / Julie Fiedler. — 1st ed.
       p. cm. — (Scary snakes)
   Includes index.
   ISBN-13: 978-1-4042-3833-6 (library binding)
   ISBN-10: 1-4042-3833-6 (library binding)
   1. Viperidae—Juvenile literature. I. Title.
   QL666.O69F54 2008
   597.96'3—dc22
                                                    2007001974

Manufactured in the United States of America

Contents

What Are Vipers?

Snakes are **reptiles** with a long, tube-shaped body covered in a skin made up of scales. Different kinds of snakes belong to groups called families. Viperidae is the family of snakes that includes both vipers and pit vipers. Together they are known as viperids. Both kinds of snakes are **venomous** and can be deadly to people and other animals.

Vipers can be less than 1 foot (30 cm) long or more than 6 feet (2 m) long. Some vipers have **patterns** on their body. They have a wide head and two large front teeth, called fangs. This book will tell you more about these scary snakes.

Viperids are found all over the world, except for Australia and Madagascar. Viperids' skin is made of scales. These scales are keeled, which means that they overlap each other, rather than being smooth.

Pit Vipers

Pit vipers have a triangular head and their eyes are almond shaped. They differ from vipers in that they have pits that sense heat on each side of their face. Pit vipers are **nocturnal**, which means they are awake at night and sleep during the day. Because they cannot see well in the dark, the pits help them hunt for **prey** and keep themselves away from **predators**.

The most common pit vipers are rattlesnakes, cottonmouths, and copperheads. These snakes all have venomous bites that can be deadly to people.

Pit

You can see the pits on this pit viper. They are on either side of its head, between the eyes and the mouth.

Fangs and Venom

Viperids have two long, hollow teeth, called fangs, that they use for biting. When a viperid bites, or strikes, its venom flows through the hollow fangs and into its **victim**. Viperids can fold their fangs back into their mouth when they do not need them.

Venom is like **saliva** made from **chemicals** in the viper's body. Venom is harmful to animals and people. Depending on the type of snake and how much venom is given in a strike, a bite may just be painful or it may be deadly.

Fangs

The fangs on this eyelash viper are folded back inside its mouth. When it is ready to bite, its fangs will fold down and outward.

Where Vipers Live

Viperids live in **habitats** such as rain forests, deserts, and mountains across Europe, Asia, and Africa. In each habitat, vipers make their homes in different places. Some dig holes in the ground and some live in trees.

Snakes are cold blooded. This means the weather has an effect on their body **temperature**. Some viperids, such as adders, **hibernate** during winter because they live in places that get cold, such as Europe. Other viperids, such as the horned viper, live in warm places, like the desert, and must dig to avoid hot sand.

Some types of viperids live in deserts. Others, like the green bush viper (inset), live in rain forests in Africa.

How Vipers Hunt

Viperids use their venom to disable or kill prey for eating. They eat small animals, such as birds, rats, and rabbits, as well as bugs, frogs, and snails. Some viperids eat other snakes.

Viperids eat their prey by using their smaller teeth to help them swallow. They can unhook their jaws, or mouthparts, to make their mouth big enough to swallow their prey whole! They can also use their venom to keep themselves safe when they feel that they are in danger. One strike from these snakes is often enough to stop whichever animal is bothering them!

Bush vipers attack their prey from trees. They hang down from the branches and catch their food by surprise! *Inset:* Snails, like the one shown here, are often eaten by viperids.

Viper Defenses

Viperids have **defenses**, such as **camouflage**, warnings, and striking. Camouflage lets an animal mix in with its habitat so that it can hide. For example, the horned viper lives in the desert and is a sandy color, which makes it hard to see against the sand.

Some viperids have warning signs to scare off predators. Puff adders can make their body bigger and hiss. Vipers can also use their fangs to bite and defend themselves when they are in danger. Russell vipers can spring forward to bite.

Horned vipers are the color of the sandy areas in which they live. This helps them both hide from their predators and creep up on their prey.

Mating and Young

Like most reptiles, most viperids lay eggs after **mating**. However, a few give birth to live young instead. This means that the baby snakes grow inside the female snake.

Viperids do not care for their young. Once they are born or hatch, or come out of their eggs, the adult snakes leave them.

As snakes grow, they outgrow their skin and must shed it. The skin often sheds in one long piece. Younger snakes, which grow quickly, shed their skin more often than older snakes. Most snakes become adults in one to five years.

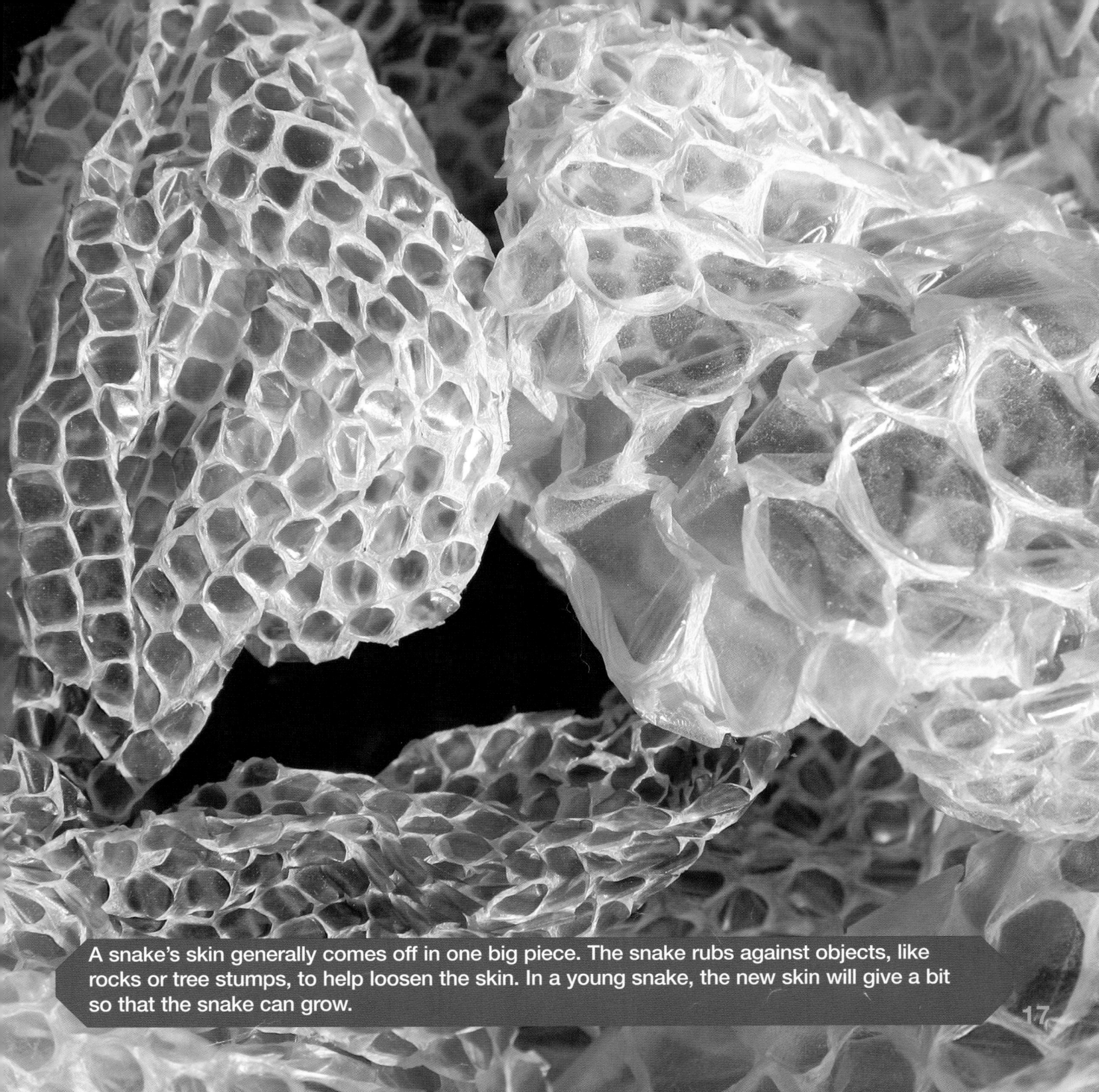

A snake's skin generally comes off in one big piece. The snake rubs against objects, like rocks or tree stumps, to help loosen the skin. In a young snake, the new skin will give a bit so that the snake can grow.

Saw-Scaled Vipers

Saw-scaled vipers are one of the deadliest vipers in the world! They are also called carpet vipers and live in Africa, India, Sri Lanka, and the Middle East. Saw-scaled vipers are very small and can grow to be about 36 inches (90 cm) long.

When saw-scaled vipers are in danger or about to strike, they move their body into a curled-up shape and rub their scales together. This makes a sizzling sound, which warns their enemies. Saw-scaled vipers can easily feel in danger and strike quickly. The fact that they are so quick to strike is one of the reasons they are so deadly.

Saw-scaled vipers are known to be quick to attack. These deadly snakes eat a wide range of prey, such as spiders, scorpions, frogs, birds, and even other snakes!

Bushmasters

Bushmasters are very **dangerous** pit vipers. Like the saw-scaled vipers, they are known to be quick to strike their victims. They are one of the longest vipers and can grow to be 8 to 12 feet (2–4 m) long! They live deep in the rain forests of Central America and South America.

Most pit vipers give birth to live young, but the bushmaster lays eggs. Females lay about 12 eggs at a time. The bushmaster is one of the few types of snakes in which the female guards her eggs. Young bushmasters have more color than adults, which are usually brown and gray with square-shaped patterns.

The bushmaster's strong venom can be deadly to people. This is because the bushmaster can inject a lot of venom with each bite and also because people are likely to be far from a hospital when bitten.

Vipers and People

Because viperids are dangerous, people must always be careful when they are near them. Some, such as the saw-scaled viper, will strike quickly, but others are not as fast or dangerous.

Viperids live throughout the world, but they live most often in places with few people around. However, bad weather, such as hurricanes, which can cause floods, can drive these snakes to areas with more people. Although they are dangerous to people, vipers can be helpful in controlling the numbers of pests such as mice. The safest place to see vipers is in a zoo!

Glossary

camouflage (KA-muh-flahj) A color or a pattern that is like one's surroundings and helps hide something.

chemicals (KEH-mih-kulz) Matter that can be mixed with other matter to cause changes.

dangerous (DAYN-jeh-rus) Can cause hurt.

defenses (dih-FENTS-ez) Things a living thing does that help keep it safe.

habitats (HA-beh-tats) The surroundings where an animal or a plant naturally lives.

hibernate (HY-bur-nayt) To spend the winter in a sleeplike state.

mating (MAYT-ing) Joining together to make babies.

nocturnal (nok-TUR-nul) Active during the night.

patterns (PA-turnz) Colors and shapes that appear over and over again on something.

predators (PREH-duh-terz) Animals that kill other animals for food.

prey (PRAY) An animal that is hunted by another animal for food.

reptiles (REP-tylz) Cold-blooded animal with scales.

saliva (suh-LY-vuh) The liquid in the mouth that starts to break down food and helps food slide down the throat.

temperature (TEM-pur-cher) The heat in a living body.

venomous (VEH-nuh-mis) Having a poisonous bite.

victim (VIK-tim) A person or an animal that is harmed or killed.

Index

Web Sites

Due to the changing nature of Internet links, PowerKids Press has developed an online list of Web sites related to the subject of this book. This site is updated regularly. Please use this link to access the list:
www.powerkidslinks.com/ssn/viper/